AGE of AQUARIUS
SPIRITUAL RECKONING

Melinda Merritt

Author's Tranquility Press
ATLANTA, GEORGIA

Copyright © 2024 by Melinda Merritt

All rights reserved. No part of this publication may be reproduced, distributed or transmitted in any form or by any means, including photocopying, recording, or other electronic or mechanical methods, without the prior written permission of the publisher, except in the case of brief quotations embodied in critical reviews and certain other noncommercial uses permitted by copyright law. For permission requests, write to the publisher, addressed "Attention: Permissions Coordinator," at the address below.

Melinda Merritt/Author's Tranquility Press
3900 N Commerce Dr. Suite 300 #1255
Atlanta, GA 30344, USA
www.authorstranquilitypress.com

Ordering Information:
Quantity sales. Special discounts are available on quantity purchases by corporations, associations, and others. For details, contact the "Special Sales Department" at the address above.

Age of Aquarius: Spiritual Reckoning /Melinda Merritt
Paperback: 978-1-964362-77-9
eBook: 978-1-964037-95-0

Contents

I Came, I Saw, I Spoke 1
The Reckoning 6
Precession of the Equinox 8
Holy Spirit Changes Things 12
The President's Role 14
Holy Spirit Whispers 15
The Age of Aquarius Will? 18
Astrology and Tree of Life 21
The Empire is Falling 24
Spirituality and Dreaming 26
The United States of America 33
Tree of Life Insights and Qualities 36
Tree of Life and United States Presidency 38
White Folkology 51
Age of Aquarius Spiritual Energy 54
Age of Aquarius Energy and You 60
Holy Spirit Equals Spirituality 63
Astrology and Spiritual Belief 65
SPIRITUAL RECKONING HAS BEGUN 69

Dedication

I dedicate this book to all who seek knowledge and are not aware of the influences that this Age of Aquarius will deliver to humanity. BE BLESSED

I Came, I Saw, I Spoke

Life is Life. This little saying is what my grandma would often say while she pondered over a situation. While I was a child, I could not grasp what she meant. Now that I am older, I do understand what it means. You can plan all you want, but if the universe has another plan, then that plan is the one which will play out. Because I have always been extremely interested in the energy and cultural development of the people in Black America, I have done an extensive developmental study of my culture and society. I called my lifelong study "The Black Evolution." This book is my summary of what I have observed.

I am a Spiritualist. What this means to me is deciding to indeed develop a committed relationship with the Creator and the Holy Spirit while living a life that would be pleasing to the Creator. For me, the Holy Spirit is the key to understanding the world. It is the feminine aspect of the Godhead and brings love and comfort to the world. More love is what we need. Of course, spirituality is not as uncomplicated as I am putting it. It takes a lifetime and then more time to get it right.

Our Spiritual journey is never ending. It is forever beginning because once you discover one level of knowledge you are introduced to another on a higher scale. Your need to know all spiritual matters is so urgent one tends to forget the life we are living. A lot of life is connecting with like minds and studying any and all written documentation available. When you begin to see that what you seek is something you have always known, the connection to your ancestors is deepened. Spirituality is the one thing that has always existed and how man and all living things are connected. One has to learn many things which make you focus on reading the Bible, praying for understanding, and mingling with people of like minds. Through spirituality, I have been able to listen to the Universe and hear what the Creator really expects of his creation.

I am in great company as a spiritualist, you see. Let me name some of the great people who were also spiritualists. Abraham, the first in the Bible to speak the knowledge of the Creator. Isaac, his son, Sarah, Abraham's wife, Moses and the Ethiopian Queen he married along with the immediate descendants of their union. Jacob, along with his descendants, were also spiritualists. Enoch, Daniel, and Noah were some of the most celebrated spiritualists who lived. Man has somehow forgotten these epic people. This human story goes on and on until man learns other polluted versions of the Creator's story. The original believers had to learn how to worship the Creator without the help of mega churches or human leaders. They were able to hear the Creator through the Holy Spirit because they did not have a television, radio, computers, and other modern-day devices. They meditated and learned to understand the symbols and hear the words of the Creator. Just think for a moment about Noah and the Ark. He had been given the messages concerning the building of the Ark through dreams, meditation, and many other symbols. He did not have a blueprint, just the command of the Creator. Mainly, they learned from the Holy Spirit of the Creator what was to be done. This makes him an undisputed Spiritualist. It was a simple thing to do in those days for those who had been selected and appointed by the Creator.

I conducted this intense cultural observation because I wanted the future generations to have some idea about their past. This past will make their future. There is a constant sociological and psychological evolution going on in the races and one must pay attention and not be led off the right path. The one thing I want people to know is that everything is connected to what happened before their present time. I examine life in the way I do because of the Sages (mother, grandma, and Maa Dove) who raised me. Their awareness of how they were genetically connected to their past was not to be overlooked. They passed to me the wisdom and knowledge they inherited from their ancestors. The Africans did not begin existing in 1619 when they arrived in America. Our ancestry goes back thousands of years. Man is just now discovering the secrets of the genes and still, know nothing of what is unknown. The genes I carry are ancient ones which began long before I ended up here at this time and place. Everyone has this same sequence of events in their own lives. Therefore, whatever you see is connected to something of the past. How does this information become relevant to this book? Well, let me tell you. The story of my existence is forever linked to the nasty slave trade in America. In my first book, <u>Merritt Magic</u>, I tried to make it very clear that all captured Africans were never to be slaves. Some of them were put here to help and tender to slaves who needed their help. My ancestors were of that lineage. The women of my heritage possessed certain unworldly qualities. I say it that way because they were able to do things which others could not. They were so strong until I had no other choice but to be as well. The Sages who raised me were brilliant women. Although they did not go to formal institutions, because circumstances would not permit, they had pure knowledge gotten from a well deeper than any man can imagine. Whenever I would ask how they knew so much about things, they would say, "it is in their blood from their ancestors." They were not entirely correct. History has now discovered that the genes of humans have a memory path of genes which will be passed down from generation to generation. This knowledge was transferred to their genes; therefore, I have them as well. It is no different from any person reading this book. You have the genes of your ancestors. Some of the knowledge given to you has been buried because you are not aware of your power. Your unseen power is the one thing that frightens the other race. They know of this power because whites witnessed it at the beginning of the slavery years. The slave owners would have heard all the tales and stories of how a Black woman would have harmed or killed other owners.

These stories would have naturally been suppressed, of course. Knowledge is a dangerous thing and to have this kind of experience out there would have damaged the slave trade in negative monetary ways. Whites, thinking themselves superior, believed they could stop this power. So, the first order of business was to make the Africans forget their inherited powers. This as done in many ways, mainly by beatings, rapes and other forms of torment. With this kind of great prolonged action, it is no wonder this knowledge went underground but never left. Some things cannot be destroyed. The "Will" of a people is one of them. I know this to be true because my grandma, Maa Dove, and my mother told me of this power hundreds of years after slavery began and "supposedly" ended. Because my parentage had little formal education, they were not able to describe, in modern-day verbiage, what they knew would happen. The Sages did, however, talk to me about what was meant by "a day of reckoning." They explained that everything in the Universe is connected and everything reacts to other things. They knew that I had a problem with the slavery issue, so by using the principles of the Universe, they sought to ease my soul and mind. To me, for another race to have kidnapped my people for slavery, was beyond sin and something which could only be handled or addressed by the Creator. The word slavery does not address what happened during that time. The personal sorrow and pain endured by the African people for such an extended period cannot be measured or handled by the mind. Maa Sis would mourn and say that the energy and soul of the people were not lost but waiting for the day of reckoning. She would laugh and say I will not see that day, but you will see the beginning of it. First, you will start to see specific signs and the things we have told you over the years will surface. All the pasts will begin to haunt that race, and they will not understand what is happening. There will be a below the surface anxiety, that will invade their subconscious thoughts. They will not know what it means or not identify it. They will feel that there is a danger approaching from somewhere. They thought that they had buried their nasty and evil ways, but just like the naked truth was buried under a stone to be forgotten, yet broke free. So will their evilness come back to reveal all? My mother would always say, "time tells all." The time is now for the "correction."

The Reckoning

"Genesis 1:14...Then God said, "Let there be lights in the firmament of heavens to divide the day from the night; and let them be for sign and seasons, and for days and years."

To have been born at such a time as this is too much to hope. I am truly blessed. What am I referring to you may wonder, well I will explain. Small towns, such as the one I grew up in, affords you a lot of time to think and watch things. One has the time to "connect the dots" as it were. There is a particular ordered system to this Universe, and one has first to be aware of this if you want to have a real shot at life. Watching the sky and its many objects at night was my best time. The night sky would always be free of clouds, and the stars would be so bright. There would be visible shooting stars with long tails. I would wonder what had caused that to happen. There would be the various clusters of stars which formed many things such as the big dipper, little dipper, the dog star and other star formations to name a few. I am an energy sensitive person. I know that human power can speak to human power without the spoken words. If you read my first book, Merritt Magic, you should be very familiar with my specialty. But in any event, I knew from my very young beginnings that the energy of the Universe has the last word on man's existence. I was aware of the impact of my energy as a child because of what my grandma, mother, and Maa Dove would have to say to me. Like one of my favorite rappers said, "you can plan a pretty picnic, but you can't predict the weather." The air, water, fire, earth are the four elements, and they can change anything you plan. So then, which energy is the most powerful? The present power which I observed on the day of the Solar Eclipse (August 21, 2017, 3:13 pm) is the Holy Spirit and the most powerful. The Holy Spirit is the reason everything appears imbalanced to us. It is not as it seems, however. See the pictures at the end of this chapter.

Precession of the Equinox

How is it that I can speak about the Age of Aquarius? How did I know about this information? I wondered about myself for many years, and now I accept that there is some knowledge in me from my ancient ancestors which nags at me to come forth. I have always known things since I was a little girl. I grew up in a world where Sages taught us regularly on otherworldly matters. They were too knowledgeable about things they should never have known. My grandma, mother, and Maa Dove were extremely knowledgeable about ancient history. They were mighty Sages and healers and were used by the Creator in many ways. That in itself is not a new thing except for the fact they were Black from the African Continent, and they kept in touch with their people, somehow, through their minds. They had no formal education and should not have known these things, except that they did. Whenever I asked how it was that they knew so much, they would say "it is in our blood." Wouldn't you know it, they were right. Genes were not discovered at that time, but they knew how knowledge was transferred. The kidnapped African people were wrongly labeled and beaten if they displayed such powers. The whites were too afraid of the thing they did not understand. But the whites cannot make ancient knowledge go away regardless of what they did. My family was one such as this. I talked about it in more detail in my other book, Merritt Magic. The knowledge which my family possesses is in the genes and will not be destroyed. The world is just discovering some of the locked secrets of the genes, but they know nothing about unseen information. Even if they saw this information, they would not recognize it. The ancient masters took time to tell us about the twelve Zodiac signs along with their meanings. I know that it was Thoth and Ma'at, his female part, which gave the civilization this knowledge. They were Egyptian and had knowledge which they had

Age of Aquarius

gained from the Creator. How was this knowledge passed down? I believe, through means unknown to man, we received this knowledge through our genes. The ancient masters give all the credit to Thoth for the many disciplines of knowledge shared with man. Astrological knowledge is the one that consumes me the most. I know that the Firmaments, the word used in the Bible to identify the Zodiac and all other heavenly bodies in the universe, is the governing body of the earth. The Firmaments were created by the Creator, of course. The Holy Spirit is the third part of the Creator, therefore, is wholly integrated into the Firmaments. So we can safely say that the Holy Spirit rules the creation. I am making this part very simple, I hope. I will not go into details but read your Bibles, you will find that I am correct. If you studied the Bible, you would see that a great deal of it speaks to the Firmaments and man's relationship which exist. In the Book of Job, for example, there are several references to the Firmaments as it relates to him and his situation. The words used are Hebrew mostly, so you would have to be knowledgeable of this fact.

For this book, we will examine how the Zodiac signs influence human beings. I am going to look at the two ways we are impacted whether we know it or not. The twelve personal Zodiac signs people use every day to define themselves are ordered as Aries, Taurus, Gemini, Cancer, Leo, Virgo, Libra, Scorpio, Sagittarius, Capricorn, Aquarius, and Pisces. To keep them in the Astrological order for births, we go clockwise on the rounded earth. To understand and stay in Universal order for time's sake, you go counterclockwise in the Zodiac Sphere to see how the Ages are displayed. Let me make myself more clear. For me to be speaking in this Age, we will order them in this manner. Gemini, Taurus, Aries, Pisces, Aquarius, Capricorn, Sagittarius, Scorpio, Libra, Virgo, Leo, and Cancer. According to the ancient Astrological experts and the people who currently keep up with the Ages, we can document this process through the information found in the Bible. You should know one crucial fact, however. The first twelve Zodiac personal signs go around the world in 365 days. The Astrological Zodiac signs complete their full turn in 24,000 to 26,000 years. Each Zodiac Age lasts between 2,000 to 2,400 years. I will explain my story this way. I am not saying, however, time begins with the story I am telling. I am only saying that this was when man became another type of expression in the creation story. I am going to demonstrate how the Bible's Spiritualists have a direct relationship with the Zodiac signs. To me, this shows how the creation and the Zodiac signs are connected and influences humanity. This also underlines the fact that the Creator is in tune with His creation.

We will start with Abraham and his wife, Sara. They were given the task of introducing LOVE into the creation. They were called out of their homeland by the Holy Spirit to go into unknown parts to spread the LOVE of God. Abraham was one of the first known Spiritualists, I think. He lived in the Age of Gemini, the sign of LOVE. Moses was a great man and a complete Spiritualist because he received his instruction through the Holy Spirit. Moses lived in the Age of Taurus. The bull represents that Age. There were no churches at that time like there are now. The Holy Spirit contacted him through the burning bush, voices from Heaven, and other means. He relied on what he learned this way. Well, he led the Jews out of Egypt and freed them. Recall the event when Moses went away for an extended period. When he returned, the people had built a golden calf or oxen or bull. (This symbol has been called all those things.) The point I am trying to make is that it represents the Age of Taurus. Taurus the bull is how we usually refer to it. The next Age is Aries. The Ram represents the Age of Aries. The ancients say this was the Age in which Jesus was born. In the Bible, Jesus is the Ram of God. When Jesus was speaking to his Disciples, He stated that He would be with them until the end of the Age. The hearers of this information thought that Jesus meant he would be here until the end of time. Historians believe that Jesus came at the end of the Age of Aries and appeared at the beginning of the Age of Pisces. You can recall when Jesus appeared to His disciples after His death. Everyone saw him and how long did he appear? How can this be explained other than a miracle? The Historians supported this conclusion with the fact that the fish represent the Age of Pisces and Jesus was the fisher of men. Fish were important while Jesus was present. The magical feeding of thousands with a small amount of fish is one story that we all know. The Age of Pisces was the paradigm used to spread the word of God to all the world. The Religion Age if you will. Too bad it has become so corrupt.

The Age of Aquarius was the next to come up. We are now in that Age. What is the confirmation? One sure way of marking the end of the Age of Pisces is the fact that there were many prominent preachers, religious leaders and the like, predicting that the end of the world was at hand. Some of them even gave the specific date and time. There was a large religious group in California who killed themselves because they felt so strongly that the end of the world was at hand. How silly were they? What is even more interesting, is that these "end of the world people" had the same feelings that the religious leaders had in the days of Jesus. They felt that the world would end as well and it was just the end of the Pisces Age. The other interesting fact is that if you examine 1600, 1700, 1800 and early 1900, there was no mention of the world coming to an end. Somehow, however, during the later 1900's, this talk became all the rage. Makes you wonder does it not.

Holy Spirit Changes Things

For people like myself born in the mid-1900's, we get to experience living at the end of the Age of Pisces and the beginning of the Age of Aquarius. How cool is that? We encountered two Ages just as Jesus. In the Bible, the symbol for Age of Aquarius is the man with the pitcher of water. Jesus associated this event with the Upper Room and in Revelations. The water being poured out is the Holy Spirit covering the earth. The pool (spirit) being poured out is what's happening now. The Holy Spirit is here and making itself known to everyone in many ways. The picture I have included, taken on August 21, 2017, is the eclipse and below it is the Spiritual Energy coming down. Even People who are not necessarily religious feel the Holy Spirit's presence, and they cannot make sense of what is going on. Some of what the Age is going to do will be corrections, cleansing, revealing all, and inviting us to join in with The Holy Spirit to make this world a better place. There is far too much hatred, corruption and evil ways here now. I am a Spiritualist, and I am always reminded that I should do more to help my fellow man, so I am writing this book. I hope people will not misunderstand my motives and join in with me and the Holy Spirit. The human race is at the bottom of many things not pleasing to the Creator, and this is our chance to make it right. As a child, the Sages who raised me told me about this time and what would happen as far as they knew. No, they did not call it the Age of Aquarius, but they knew that a significant change would occur and they wanted me to be alert. In America, the slavery issue is the elephant in the room, so to speak. White people prefer not talking or acknowledging it. They feel that if they leave it out of the books in schools, this will help their situation. I beg to differ. We will have to deal with this horrible thing if America is to survive. White America cannot do what they did to the kidnapped Africans and expect no karma. The Africans were innocent, highly disrespected, and mistreated for greed. It was a significant case of redistribution of wealth in the history of this country. Did you think that the Creator would give a pass on it because America said it was a Christian Nation? Some things will not disappear just because you refuse to acknowledge it. This correction will be a part of this Age. Enough on that for now. This book is just the first part of a series so stay tuned.

The President's Role

Merritt and Mays was the name of our family's grocery store. My father and his sister, Aunt Bessie, had a very lucrative business for many years at that location. My father owned that building as well as other properties around the town. You have to remember, my father started his business in the late 1940's when the white race truly disrespected Black people. My father and I had a close relationship. He was happy to teach me about life, including his businesses. Being around the store and other places with him showed me the importance of numbers. He was always counting something or doing something with numbers. He would say, "the world is built on some number system, so you better know your numbers". My father was a self-made successful business man with only a third-grade education. I soon discovered that my love for Astrology and numbers worked very well together. The importance of knowing these two things began my journey for the quest of ancient knowledge and connecting the dots of humanity as I knew it. My father gave me a valued representation of a father who leads and looks out for all concerned. The role of the President is to lead a Country with respect and dignity. In America, the President should serve all the citizens fairly as the law permits. This president is missing some key skills and the people are paying the price. This president does not have honor in his being.

Holy Spirit Whispers

Laying outside in our backyard counting the stars as a child, allowed me to know where and when certain changes would take place. There is no title for what I do, just some inner knowledge which gives me the understanding. There would be different formations of the stars according to the time of year and I kept track of such things. I would frequently observe shooting stars which would fascinate me to no end. I watched them until they were no longer visible to me. I thought that they fell to earth at some point, I knew not where, however. I rarely see these shooting stars these days. I wonder what caused them to stop? My grandma would tell us what a particular shooting star meant and she would always be correct. The firmaments had a lot to do with the weather and growth of the crops, and other such things as this. Grandma knew how the energy of the heavenly bodies affected the energy on earth. When I saw certain formations, I knew what would be happening on earth. I have always written down the things I saw and when I was introduced to certain knowledge later in life, I could understand it even though I am unfamiliar with the information. It seems that I got some kind of knowledge that only surfaces when I have an energy encounter. Most times this memory is triggered by energy words and sometimes it is an object. To understand this thing took me a long time and much study. I have studied ancient knowledge since I first went off to college in 1969. I knew that if I wanted to understand the world, I now find myself, I need ancient knowledge. Everything is connected and I wanted to "connect the dots". In January 2018 at 3:00 A.M., I was awakened from a sound sleep and went to the window to see if something outside had caused this. The first thing I noticed was that the sky was lighter than it should be, not dark at all. The sky appeared like it was almost dawn.

There were plenty of stars on a pinkish background. I had seen this type of sky just one other time as a child. This meant that there was a very bright heavenly body somewhere I could not see. Something like a distant Moon. There was no Moon. This also meant that an alignment of Heavenly bodies was taking place causing the strangeness. I just started to pray because the Creator was opening up doors of information to be released to the earthly creatures. Suddenly, I started thinking about the number nine (9). I began to wonder why this number was present in my head. I began seeing nines all over the place. I am a Master Tarot Card Reader, so I knew what the number meant in that arena. This was unusual for me to single out one number while not giving a reading. I began to pray for clarity. I dreamed about it later that morning because this number nine was very "loud" in my head. I concluded this after the Universe confirmed it through a spiritual message I watched later that morning. In case you are unaware, the Universe finds ways to confirm things to you if you just listen and pay attention. The current 45th President (I try not to say his name because I think it would be a sin) in the White House is the nine. The number 4+5 can be reduced to the number nine. The number nine I had screaming in my head is about this President. One definition of nine in the ancient world was for the number of gods in Egypt and other kingdoms. This president certainly has the belief that he is a god. He conducts himself in this mindset. When in actuality, I think he is the "Emperor who has no clothes" kind of president. Just as everything else in life, the numbers have a positive or negative side to them. For this president, unfortunately, the negative side is what we are seeing. He is a man who lives by a negative set of morals. He has expressed this himself in many ways, and I am only repeating what is already known. Another important meaning of the number nine (according to the Biblical Tree of Life) is the foundation, with the influence of the Moon. For this country, the president should represent, in many ways, the foundation. Again, it could be a negative or positive thing. For us in this country, it is not going to be good. The president can strengthen or weaken a foundation in the land he rules. So far, the 45th President is the absolute negative force as everyone Is now finding out. He has already shaken many foundations which people hold dear, and he has done it in record time. It is happening so fast that most people are not aware of it yet. Don't worry, however, he will not disappoint. The man is suffering from a serious mental disorder which will only get worse. I predict that by the end of 2018, he will have a total meltdown from which he will not recover. The 40th president had the same mental problem, but the media was not allowed to speak on it. I knew it because I saw the energy problem that always surrounded him when he was allowed out in public and knew it. Also, he had a very clever wife who covered expertly for him. The 45th president has a porn star wife (based on her naked pics on FB) which will not be so clever. The world can easily see that they are not a "happy couple". More importantly, however, he was raised on that cultural inherited hatred created at this country's establishment.

The Age of Aquarius Will?...

Because this is the Age of Aquarius, a serious revealing and cleansing time in man's existence, how will the earth be impacted by the Holy Spirit? Mainly, this Spiritual Age is a balancing time as some Planets change positions thereby shifting the energy fields. As we have noted, in each Age prior to this one, something huge happened in humanity. What really will happen is the question on many awakened minds. The last time this Age was "front and center" happened over 25,000 to 30,000 years ago. Is this the very first time this Age has appeared or were there others? How many times has it been seen by humans? Were there civilizations knowledgeable enough to record the happenings of the stars at that time? If there were this kind of records kept, where can they be found? This information is unknown to me. There may have been people who were as evil and developed as we are. With the cleansing, which is done by the Age of Aquarius, the Natural Law balancing which occurred may have ended their time altogether. There is no way to know yet. The one thing I do know, however, is that the Universe has strong Natural Laws and they have become severely unbalanced. There will be a correction which means destruction in many ways. This is the day of reckoning my grandma told me about. She would say, "I won't be here for that part, but you will see it". "My job is to prepare you to recognize it when it happens". My grandma, Maa Sis, was a very powerful Sage. We spent many hours watching the skies at night as she would talk about what was to come (this Age) and other things. I wondered how she knew so much since she never had a formal education of any kind. She would say, "it is in your blood, child". Even with that statement, she was not too far off. Genes had not been discovered at that time, yet she knew that the information had been handed down from generation to generation.

If you read my other book <u>Merritt Magic</u>, you will read a lot about her. The three elements of air, fire, and water have already caused all kinds of unusual weather situations, thereby, drastically affecting the fourth element, earth. It is cold when it should be hot. It is snowing when the Sun should be shining, etc. The people, as are all living things, are being negatively impacted as a direct result. For my readers of the Bible, you should be aware of all the references to the Stars and the Cosmos as it relates to governing the earth. I call it the Holy Spirit speaking. For me, to be able to witness such happenings is more exciting than I could say. I truly understand a lot of what Is happening and about to happen. This Age has already revealed many unknown facts concerning the weather and we are perplexed. The weather is a perfect example of how the energy of the Cosmos affects the energy on earth. The people who study the Cosmos, professionally or privately, have noticed many new events. One thing I have recently seen and watched very closely is the blinking of Stars. One night while observing the sky and focusing on some regions of Stars, I thought I saw some stars blink on and off. I had seen this some two years earlier but paid little attention. I live in the rural area, so I have many nights to watch clear skies full of stars. The first time I noticed it, I thought it was a problem with my telescope. However, the next night the same thing happened. Now, it happens just about any time the Stars are visible which means that this action has intensified. What could such activities mean? They blink in different areas at different times. It reminds me of Christmas tree lights. I feel about them as I did the Shooting Stars. I am fascinated and thrilled to see such a phenomenon. I know this is something which is essential, I do not know how to define it. Anything that happens in the Cosmos impacts the earth. For some unknown reason, studying and thinking about the blinking star thing, made me curious about something related to numbers and Astrology. I had a thought come to me about the history of the United States. In light of this revelation, I did something I never had before. I studied the history of the United States Presidents. I decided to look at their number sequence as it relates to Spirituality. I wanted to know if there was any relationship between their election order number and the Biblical Tree of Life numbers and definitions. In doing so, I found some very intriguing facts concerning a relationship with those selected. Let me first tell you who they are and then explain why I was impressed and interested to see the ties. They are President Abraham Lincoln, 16th, President George W. Bush, 43rd, President John F. Kennedy, 35th, President Lyndon B. Johnson, 36th, President Richard Nixon, 37th, President Bill Clinton, 42nd, President Barack Obama, 44th, and lastly the current 45th, President. Because this current president is a negative nine, we will wait to see how the foundation will hold up. The impact to the foundation will be negative and not at all spiritual. He has only been in office for 365 days and we have had more turmoil coming from him than any other president that I have known. Actually, he is the catalyst which was necessary to bring out the negative things to shake up the foundation of the United States. He was not to win this election because the numbers were not on his side. Not even he or his people thought he would win. Yet, he did win because the Universe ordained it to begin the foundation change. It is time for something new, different, and of course, better for this Country and the world.

Astrology and Tree of Life

I first found out about the Tree Of Life in the 80's when I began studying ancient Jewish knowledge and other esoteric material. I studied many spiritual pools of knowledge including the Bible. The more I read about the Tree of Life and its importance to the Garden of Eden and the Creator, I clearly realized that the numbers represented "weighted wisdom" words of old. The hidden knowledge attached to the meaning of a number became an entrance into an ancient way of thinking about truth, understanding, and spirituality. It was as though a magical door opened and I entered. Door openings are very significant in the Astrology world. It is through door openings in the Cosmos this knowledge is passed into the world we now live. These door openings are spoken about in many ancient sacred books and writings. For example, there are four documented Astrological door openings. These four openings happen at the same time every year, so they are fixed. These door openings happen in the four months of March 21+, June 21+, September 21+, and December 21+. I used the "+" after each number to indicate that the door opening stays open more than one day. The truth is that it is unthinkable for a man to be completely accurate on how it starts and end. The happenings in the Cosmos take time to complete. As it so happens, my mother, grandma, my brother Phil, and myself all were born during a door opening. How does this fact play into our "knowing", I cannot say. I just know that we all have special qualities no one else had. Once I was introduced to Qabalah, the Tree of Life took on another form of enlightenment. The wisdom and knowledge I found were more important than anything else. It seems to open up many different levels of understanding as relates to the Creator and the Heavenly Host. Once I understood how important numbers were in Qabalah, father's teachings took on a deeper awareness and importance. How wise was my father, who only had a third-grade education, very? The study of Qabalah has many aspects and levels of knowledge, so it takes a lifetime to come to terms with it. Honestly, however, I do not think one could ever learn all there is to know about Qabalah, but we love the enlightenment it affords us. For me, it helps provide Spiritual order, clarity, and meaning to life. My purpose for this book is to examine the spiritual meanings of the ten Sephira spheres on the Tree of Life as related to the selected US Presidents. The Tree of Life has ten identified spheres with spiritual meaning attached to the assigned number. A vast amount of information can be gained about a person using their birthday spiritual number. It is so interesting how accurate people's actions fit their spiritual life/birth path numbers. In my tarot card readings, the spiritual life path number will always appear. Should you want to know your spiritual life/birth path number, it is easily done. There is but one way to get the spiritual life path number, and that is by adding your birthday numbers together and reducing it down to a single number digit. Once the signal number is identified, meaning can be gained by using the Tree of Life spiritual number matching. When the birthday is reduced down to the single digit, this number becomes your spiritual life/birth number. It is fixed for life. Qabalah will reduce your complete birthday to a number between one and ten. The matching number on the Tree of Life has a particular meaning which will have characteristics that a person can easily identify in themselves. Any person or event which has a number associated with it can usually be reduced and measured using this Tree of Life method. Yes, I have studied the Kabbalah knowledge for many years and still, cannot claim to be an expert. I am, however, well versed in the various principles and can deduce and connect as well as anyone who calls themselves an expert. In this discipline, it is the use of intellect and ancient wisdom which will get you from one level to another. There will always be something else to learn. For me and my grandma, mother and Maa Dove, "it is in the blood". This means that I usually connect very easily with the introduction of some new knowledge. Most of the time the information appears as pictures in my head or energy field.

Somehow, I knew that I already carried this information. The presentation of the words only awakened what was there asleep. Now, let us explore these findings by using the legacy of a person with strong spiritual courage, Dr. Martin Luther King, Jr. Dr. Martin Luther King, Jr. was born on 01-15-1928 (1+1+5+1+9+2+8=27; 2+7=9). So Dr. King's spiritual life/birth path number is nine. On the Tree of Life, the nine represents the completion of a cycle, judgment, change in the foundation, and the birth of a new way of looking at things and ideas. The number nine is also linked to childbirth (a new life) since it takes nine months for completion of the birth cycle. These things and more did Dr. King certainly bring onto the world stage and America. He used his spirituality to open up the eyes for many who could not see. His spirituality gave birth to new ideas and gave hope to many people who were ignored and bullied. He made the Black people have the kind of pride never before seen in such large numbers. He showed courage against great opposition. He lived up to his spiritual life number Nine. He gave his life for his spiritual belief. Dr. King's legacy will be remembered until the end of time. He chose the positive side of his spiritual life number. We could also choose the negative side as well. like the 45th.

DR. MARTIN LUTHER KING, JR., WAS THE GREATEST MAN IN OUR LIFETIME.

The Empire is Falling

The fall of the Roman Empire has always brought certain questions to mind. One such question is whether or not the population was aware of the crumbling world around them. What would be the definite signs to alert everyday citizens? Were there people somewhere recording the demise to be left for future generations? What were the formations of the Cosmos at this time? The Romans had a high intellect at that time, so I know that someone was thinking along the lines of signs and wonders. Was there an Astrologer in his offices recording the movement of the Heavenly Hosts? It is so true when people say "the only thing constant is change". When the change of energy first occurred in the Cosmos and began to interact with the Empire's energy, did anyone notice? What of Sodom and Gomorrah? Was there an alert to what was about to happen? Were they so secure in their acts because nothing bad had happened to stop them from their decline. Was there no Dr. Martin Luther King, Jr., present to warn them that they were headed down the wrong path when they needed him? Is there someone now recording the changes in our world for the United States. I know there is going to be a very profound change in our world, do you? I don't know what Heavenly Hosts member was present at those times of destruction, but I know it ruled the day in the fall of the Roman Empire and the other cities. The energies of the Roman Empire were severely out of balance and the energy of the governing bodies of the Cosmos will win every time. There have been many civilizations modeled after the Roman Empire because of its "seemingly" success. This fall just represents that things are not always what they seem. The United States is certainly one example of where their model was used. Change in the Cosmos takes time to be felt on earth, so people's immediate action can take a moment to be corrected. The old saying of one gets back what he puts out is at play here. The Age of Aquarius is in full effect and will bring about major changes here on earth.

Spirituality and Dreaming

Here, I want to tell you about a dream that I had many times. I am a serious dreamer and I have always understood their importance. Blame it on my heritage, but I know that dreaming is one way your ancestors communicate with you. My ancestors speak to me all the time through my dreams. Dreaming is also a way that the Creator communicates with His people. There are a lot of Blacks who have this heritage but because of the horrible event that happened to us, a lot of us have forgotten our abilities, "temporally". This Age will balance and correct this minor breakage as well. Get ready my Black sisters. This particular dream takes place in a beach-like area and we are facing a vast ocean. At first, it was my mother and I standing together talking. We are under a fixture which looks like an overhead bridge or something. There are other people there but not near us. They are visible all along the beach area as far as I can see. We all are facing the ocean watching this extremely large wall of water far out in the ocean. We can tell that it is far far away but it is still very large, roaring noisily, and moving towards us. My mother, whose nature is not to worry and trust in the Creator, is speaking softly to me telling me not to worry because it will be alright. She touches my face and brush my hair and smiles lovingly. She always says, "it is here and we knew it would come. Don't worry, it will be alright". We then just stand to look at the moving wave of water. I see the foam at the top and feel the breeze. The first few times I had the dream both my mother and sister were alive. My mother passed away in 1993, and I still had the dream. The last few times I had the dream, my sister, who had also passed some years after mother, joined us. She did not speak nor did she seem afraid. We all were very calm. The dream is always the same. Upon awakening, I am never panicky or alarmed. The emotions a

26

person feels during the dream and upon awakening from a dream is very important. It can tell you quite a lot about the dream. To wake calm means that the balance is present and it is a positive one. The next thing to be done is interpret the scene. The fact that the water wall was so large and there were other unfamiliar people included means it was not just about me and mother. I knew that this water would cover the entire earth surface. I knew it was a very spiritual dream and from the Creator because of the huge amount of water. This reoccurring dream was the main indicator, for me, that we are in the Age of Aquarius. I say this because this Age is about pouring spiritual water over the earth's surface. The very first time I heard of the Age of Aquarius was when a Black singing group called The Fifth Dimensions made a song about it. The name of the song was "The Age of Aquarius" and about the arrival of this Age coming up very soon. This was in the late 1960's, early 1970's. The song just never left my head and my interest grew from there. There are no coincidences. I was listening to hear that song at that time. All throughout life, I have met and interacted with this Age of Aquarius energy in one form or another. I understand so much about it and can't explain why. Well, that is not completely true. I was told a lot of things about this Age as a child. I did not remember those talks until a few years ago. Then things started happening quickly in the past five years. I also have studied the Heavenly Hosts all my life and can tell by the energy which is currently on earth that a major change is about to happen. There has been such an intensity in the energy here which signals a major change. This Age is considered a very humanitarian era and will do much for balancing and correction in this area. When a nation such as America is rising up, there is much humanity that is lost. In the case of America, they have never had a good humanitarian principle from its beginning. They have what they presented as humanitarian acts but this was only a front. Everything here is based on hatred, making money, and greed. The United States was built on a fake foundation which means that there was never a solid foundation to build a great country. Despite what is stated about the origin of this Country, the people who came and had the most influence were the people who left Europe because they wanted to practice a sick, strict form of religion. This is where the horrible control devil came in, cast its net, took over, and began the downfall of America before it was off the ground. They tried to pass these evil works off as Christianity while still retaining the sick evil control. You cannot be a Christian nation and treat the original owners of the land and the stolen African people in such inhuman ways and love the Creator. You are only fooling yourself. America has tried to pretend that there was nothing wrong with their evil actions. The descendants of the white race today believe their forefathers were right. Their forefathers were completely wrong, of course. The whites became so arrogant, superior thinking, and heartless, they have forgotten that what goes up must come down. America cast their dye for destruction with the attempted destruction of the American Indian and the awful, cruel, most inhuman treatment of the Africans they kidnapped. There are some "karma" things happening to a lot of the descendants of the white race which kidnapped the African people. Suddenly these people are having unseen, yet heard, notifications. Ever since the people from Africa came to this Country, the whites have been teaching hate towards us for no reason. Whites who subscribe to such teachings will always show a negative display. These displays are becoming more and more assertive. A great example would be all the white men shooting and killing a lot of people for no apparent reason. These notifications show themselves in the form of an unclear silent voice in the back of their physical minds. This voice is becoming louder and louder in their heads. It is causing fear, on many levels, to surface and cause much trouble and sadness for people. Some of this trouble has taken on harmful actions such as suicide, deep levels of depressions, complete mind dissolving, just to name a few. Most of the descendants choose to ignore the message because some do not understand it and some believe that their superior whiteness will protect them. They believe they have nothing to worry about because they are white. There will be a correction and balance for their negative actions. The people who did this to the African people always thought that there would be nothing done to them because of their actions. They are wrong because of the One who governs, "Cause and Effect" For every action, there is a reaction. These principles never change. It may take some time for this to be seen, but it will happen. Look how long the Jews were in captivity, but the change happened and Egypt was punished. My grandma told me a lot about the happenings to come in this Country, but I think we should just wait to see the madness unfold. Really, this unfolding is in full effect. I stated somewhere earlier that the 45th President was chosen by the forces that rule this planet. He was not to win according to reports up until the last minute. Yet he won. The forces that rule have decided to make many changes on this planet and luckily for us, we get to see some of them. The 45th was just the catalyst for these fundamental changes because he will help the evil to be known in untold ways. Evil follows evil, if you will. He is evil and the majority of his followers are evil. Just as President Lincoln was the catalyst used to free the Africans, the 45th will be used to bring evilness to its final conclusion. When in actuality, it was the spirituality of the African people who caused this to happen. Their strong will to be free and the connections to the ancestral spirits that travel with them from Africa and other places. The 45th is perfect for this role because he is negative in humanitarian practices, has a petty KKK attitude, unsophisticated view of women, and an out-of-control deviant sexuality has helped to raise the curtain on all that is being exposed right now. At this time in history, the negative sexual behavior of the white men is being exposed all over the place. Every day there is a bigger and more horrid sexual misbehavior brought forth in the United States. This drama will continue to unfold because the worst is yet to come out.

During the terrible years of the captured people of Africa, the white man used the beautiful Black female to express his nasty sexual behavior. These men had no limits and showed no mercy to the Black woman. They even had a pet name for us, "belly-warmers," Even calling us whores after raping us. This is part of the reason the Judgment has come. One of the most important thoughts for me is, how is it that white people thought they could cause so much misery to a people who had done nothing to provoke them. Such redistribution of human wealth with no negative returns is how whites see their acts. Well, they are wrong. The motivation for sex, money, and control has invited this setback or correction and possible demise of the US. People have forgotten the misery that these women endured with death being their only relief. I have not forgotten them. I speak for them because their souls are not at rest. They are happy about all this exposure, however, but not quite finished with the behind-the-scenes actions. For now, they are delighted that the white man is on display for his sexual misbehavior. They are helping from behind the scenes to ensure that all is exposed. White people do not understand what I just said because they are not from ancient people like Africans. The whites do not believe what they cannot see and that makes it more fun for people like me to watch. People like me who know about spirits and the power they possess. The fun has just begun. The whites do not have a clue why these things are happening, but I do. How is it that I can make such statements of this kind? Well for many reasons, such as logic, a study of sacred documents, specific cause and effects applications and knowing how the Universe works. But mostly, however, because my grandma, Maa Sis, and Maa Dove told me about it. If you are unfamiliar with Maa Sis, and Maa Dove, then you need to read my other book, <u>Merritt Magic.</u> These ladies were influential Sages of African descent, and they knew how to use their gifted powers. There is specific knowledge which has been passed down to the African population, especially the Black woman, which gives us access to sacred knowledge. My grandma and the other Sages believed it to be in their blood. They were not entirely wrong, however. The discovery of genes was years away at that time. As it turns out, these genes contain more information than the color of your hair and eyes. They contain material which has yet to be discovered. But the white man is the chief investigator of the gene, and he is not equipped to know about such information. Thank the Creator for my heritage. I do not have to wait that long. I already know. Besides, I will probably be dead before the discovery arrives. Not that I am ready now to die, it just will take a long time for them to figure it all out. How does one prove that an event was regulated/governed by a particular discipline? One of the things done by the Heavenly Host is ruling our region Could that be scientifically proven, I think so.? The answer is, you cannot. In the year 79 AD, it is recorded that the cities of Pompeii and Herculaneum were destroyed in real time because it happened so quickly. These cities were prosperous and a part of the Roman Empire. The cities were in the proximity of the Vesuvius volcano. Just imagine, people and their families had been living in that area for many generations. I am sure that there had been rumbling on occasions from the huge volcano. Nothing happened, and nothing happened the next time nor the next. For many many years, this process probably went on. Then one day it happened. It is recorded that at least twenty feet of ash covered the two cities quickly. Suddenly there was no one or nothing else. I wish I could someday see the Heavenly Hosts charted for that event. The volcano was governed by them and to see that formation of heaven would make me very happy. The site was hidden and very well preserved when discovered in 1599. To the researcher's amazement, the things were undisturbed and much intact. People had died doing regular daily chores. Something strange to find and the researchers went down in history for such a great rescue of historical evidence. The governing bodies totally destroyed the cities and why did they deserve this? The cities of Sodom and Gomorrah were too destroyed for all their sexual imbalance and wicked sexual abuse. Were such things happening in Pompeii which would also cause the destruction of the two cities? I think so because these were wealthy and successfully advanced societies. This type of sexual deprivation of self-respect and others seems to travel with the advancement of humans.

The United States of America

As a Black female born in 1950, I grew up in a society which taught that the white man and white people were superior and all the power belonged to them. White society went all the way in making sure we received less than human treatment. White folks are just bullies and terrorists not superior. I think this Is why they hate other terrorists from other countries because they are the same kind. By adopting this "superior" attitude, whites felt that they could treat us any way they liked. Such is the segregated world in which we lived. The extent to which whites would go to ensure we knew this, was countless. This isolated attitude took on a life of its own. It became a vicious animal which lives on to this day. Imagine this, everywhere you go and encounter white people, male or female, hatred is always present. A Black person was expected to "know their place." What the hell did that mean, I could never figure out. I took it to say that I was too powerful to be in their presence. I always thought white people who treated me with undo hatred were really silly and very insecure. I tried my best to stay out of their world as much as possible. The white people who are here now do not know why they hate us. They are just doing as taught. The thing about hatred is this; you cannot control it. You can tell your off-spring to hate Blacks, Jews, etc. but this hatred will spill over into other areas. The accidental mass shootings are now happening as a by-product of this hatred being passed down. The world of whites are wondering what is causing this, how can it be stopped? They refuse to acknowledge that years of being taught to hate has produced the off-springs that they now produce. They can stop what is happening now to them if they would teach love instead of hate. They believe that they have the power to control human nature, but they do not as our spiritual will continue to show them. The very sad thing that the whites in America.

What I have done is to teach hatred as a normal thing. It is not. It goes against the Holy Spirit. Love and hate are the same life highway we travel, but with love, you go forward and hate you go backward. Look at how America has become a bed of corruption, killings, sexual abuse, and lack of respect for the women., just to name a few. Hate did this. This Country has been ruled by white men who don't have the spiritual knowledge to run a Country such as America. They believed that the "superior" nature that they adopted is all they need to be successful. When this claim is just a bully attitude Bullies always crash and burn and how happy am I to witness the beginnings of this change. To understand what is happening right now in America, one must visit the past to know how things got this way. Nothing happens overnight in the real world, because everything is connected to a previous action. In America, sadly enough, most events of a cultural and/or government nature are directly or indirectly related to the slavery issue. And it goes without saying, that everything is connected to events that happened before. In this Age of Aquarius, we get to see some significant results of the establishment and growth of this Country. I wonder if there have been other civilizations that were able to observe such a thing. I was born at the end of Pisces Age and now live in the Age of Aquarius. How cool is that? One has to remember, however, that an Age can last from 2200 to 2500 years. The United States appeared near the end of the Pisces Age, which is sometimes referred to as "Age of Religion" if you will. The Christian world agrees that Jesus was here some 2000+ years ago due to the Age of Pisces. In actuality, it is believed that Jesus lived at the end of Age of Aries and on into the beginning of the Pisces Age. In fact, this Age of Pisces was definitely the period in which religion was created, outlined, and enforcement implemented in the human race. Do keep in mind. Spirituality has always been here, long before religion. I am sure that all who read and understand this book will agree that things have not gone too well in that religion department. Due to corruption, greed, grab for power and other human negatives.

People are now awakening to the need to be spiritual, not religious. I make no assertions about other races and their definition and understanding of their existence, but I do know they are perplexed when it comes to Black women and our heritage. I have studied my race from the beginning of my entrance into this period until now. You see, I believe the essence and energy of a person live on and on. That energy and spirit can reenter based on a principle man has yet to comprehend. The power of Jesus, John Brown (born a slave as result of rape), and Dr. Martin Luther King, Jr., have been reappearing for generations as needed. These are just a few examples. I know there will be some who disagree with me, but it doesn't matter. Those who doubt cannot change what is true. I say this with absolute certainty because of the many Black female souls I have encountered during my life. They are the souls of the unfortunate captured Africans who did not have the opportunity to be heard or seen. These souls will appear through the birth of new life. There will be an untold number of Black kids born with extraordinary abilities and skills. The appearance of the "old souls" will become more apparent all over the world and especially in America shortly. To be honest, this return entrance has already begun. The Age of Aquarius is about many humanitarian acts and deeds with spiritual correction and balancing being just two. Other races will never comprehend what I have just said because they are not of African heritage. The Sages, who raised me, explained how some things would come about at this time, and not to panic. One such happening was that souls do not just disappear when the body ceases to live. The souls of a particular heritage will always remain, if not in one generation, then in another. The one sure thing that the other races have learned about the Black woman is that she will not be ignored and that there Is no one stronger in spirit, heart, and will. The white man is destroying himself trying to destroy us. How ironic life has become.

Tree of Life Insights and Qualities

The Kabbalah Tree of Life represents man's spiritual representation of the macrocosm and microcosm connection between God, the universe and man. It is the spiritual realm designed to restore harmony to His Creation. Each of the ten spiritual Sephirot is assigned definitions explaining the influence and power of each. In this book, I will use four spiritual Sephirot associated with human attributes to show how God can use a man for His Divine purpose. The four Sephirot are Tiphareth (6), Sphere of the Sun; Netzach (7), Sphere of Venus; Hod (8), Sphere of Mercury; and Yesod (9), Sphere of the Moon. The Six Sephira represents the association with the Son of Man as well as the Sun. Also, the man was created on the six day of Creation which further explains the influence. Netzach, seven Sephiroth, depicts spiritual victory, harmony in existence, Emperor mindset, Daleth (Astrological door opening), acts as a sword and the right foot of God. It is also a sphere of kindness, puts things in motion, humanitarian, strong sense of community, and is on the pillar of mercy. Hod, eight Sephiroth, depicts glory, spiritual splendor, strength, and strong humanitarian convictions. Amplifies complexity and intricacy in existence and is on the pillar of severity. Strong sense of community, justice, and considered the left foot of God which puts things in motion. The seven and eight Sephirot work together to do the Divine Will of God. The Sephirot is one way to illustrate the Creation communication with humankind. Yesod, Ninth Sephira, represents a severe influence. It represents judgment, foundation, as well as, is considered to be a Godly number in ancient societies, describes a two-edged sword, and identifies with reproductive organs. This number is more controlled by the Heavenly Hosts, the Moon more particularly. Surely, you have noticed the increased appearances of the Moon within the past year or two. It seems that every phase of the Moon is competing for time and space. This Moon increase causes plenty of that intense energy which has kept things on edge and volatile. The Moon's power directly affects the water and emotions in our body. Don't believe me, go to an ocean and watch how the Moon impacts the water. The spiritual relationship that exists between the seven, eight and ninth Sephirot is known as the Astral triad. You see, they govern the background processes and hidden mental systems of the universe and its denizens which cannot ordinarily be detected.

Tree of Life and United States Presidency

Now, I will examine the relationship between the selected President's spiritual leadership number and the Kabbalah's Tree of Life's definition associated with each of these numbers. Hopefully, you will see the Astrological and spiritual connections between them. To understand the entire meaning of the definitions, you have to think conceptually. Sometimes, you have to resist the narrow definition of meaning and go to a higher frame of reference. The last thing is, remember that the universe operates on a dual system, the old positive and negative syndrome. Now let's see what happens.

The first of these is President Abraham Lincoln, the 16th President, (1861-1865). His spiritual leadership path number is (1+6=7) seven. The meaning for seven is Victory, influenced by plant Venus; Emperor minded; and Daleth (astrological door opening). President Lincoln was the catalyst used for this humanitarian mission from God. What did God need him to do? The freeing of the African people in America. I read somewhere that President Lincoln did not want to free the slaves but felt that this would be necessary to win the Civil War. I believe that he worried and resisted what the universe wanted him to do about the Africans. Think about this, the massive "redistribution of wealth" (which is what slavery was) made white men very wealthy and powerful. This slave trade was something that the South and many others did not want to end. All the raping, humiliations, and money earned off the Africans evoked much opposition if someone tried to stop it. White men were having too much fun with the cruelty to Black women and would do anything in their power to continue. So much so, they were willing to kill each other, destroy their life and any other thing, so that it would not cease. This opposition expressed itself in the form of a Civil War. Here you find a sick bunch of people, hate, hate. and more hate. The slavery issue was the most significant controversy of that day. It continues to haunt America to this day. It will never go away because there was too much damage done to an innocent race of people. President Lincoln finally did sign the document ending slavery not knowing that the decision was not his alone. I think he did understand that they were made by the governing bodies of the Heavenly Hosts. I am not saying that Lincoln loved the Africans, it is just that his spirituality guided him down the right path. I believe that this deep-down spirituality ruled his heart and actions. I am also sure, knowing that if he did this act, death would surely come. He would never have done it on his own. It took courage to gain this victory, yet he did. He was following the powers governed by the Heavenly Hosts. The universe, not man, claimed the victory. The devil did respond to this courage act by beginning a cultural inherited hatred which exists in full force to this day. Some of the known expressions of this hate is segregation, hate groups from the lowly kind to the White House, and individual expressions. Anywhere there are white people in America, you can find one kind of hate or another. I want people to know that I do not hate the white folk, I just want them to stop their hate. I am a Black lady telling her story of the world in America.

The second President for the examination is the 43rd President, Georgia W. Bush (2001-2009). His spiritual leadership number, (4 + 3 = 7) is seven. Although the same qualities apply to this seven, the outcome was not on the positive side. The victory he sought never arrived. His spirituality had been buried too deeply under the weight of the culturally inherited hatred to help him. Not to worry, he is not alone. Many people of that race have buried their spirituality so deeply it will not surface. Unlike during President

Lincoln's time, segregation and white issues of superiority were not as pronounced. However, the Civil War, which began at the time of President Lincoln, was when and how inherited hatred took root in this County. President George W. Bush grew up surrounded by the elements of that hate, white superiority, and bigotry, as we all know. I know this to be true because I grew in his generation. Just as President Lincoln, myself, and others, Bush was born with spirituality, but he was not strong enough to prevent its burial. President George W. Bush's home life, while growing up, was not comfortable. He and his father were never at ease. The son was rebellious and fought back at his father whenever the opportunity appeared. But in reality, the son was fighting back because he resolved to deny his true self to be included and accepted in his white world. After all, for white folk to be kicked out of the KKK and other such groups, was not to be considered. Although he was very wealthy, he was not very successful, and his father always reminded him. He felt like a failure in his father's eyes for most of his life. Then, the golden opportunity appeared. He could become President of the United States. So it happened, he became the 43rd President. The presidency did not go well. He found this job very hard with a lot of controversy and scandal. I can't remember anything significant President Bush accomplished before the war in the Middle East. After the attack on the Twin Towers on September 11, 2001, his presidency was on a slow downward slope. This unnecessary war is still going on seventeen years later. The victory he sought again eluded him. He left after eight years in office yet a failure in his father's eyes. For the loss of some 4,000 lives in America, Bush has killed millions. He was a man who needed and sought a victory to make his father proud of him. He was unable to gain the victory. This tension does not mean, however, that no love was between them. I am sure they did love each other. The last time I saw President Bush live on television, I was able to study his energy and concluded that he was sad and torn. He is sad and does not know how to fix his heart. He could die an unfulfilled man and empty of his true feelings. There is still hope for some things to change for the better for him, I believe. This energy on the earth right now can work miracles if we allow it. The problem white people are facing at this very moment is the lack of spirituality and denial. The fact that so much time is spent teaching their children cultural inherited hatred, means that the true spirituality we are born with is being crushed and sent away never to return. I am sure that some whites share my thoughts and feelings, but can't break rank to change things. To solve any problem involves three steps; to identify the question, define and resolve, you cannot raise children to hate Blacks, Jews, Mexicans and all non-whites, while also teaching them how to love their guns. What you end up with are mentally unbalanced children who cannot manage their reactions inwardly. The world can now see some of the results of these cultural inherited hatred teachings being played out in real time. The increase in teenage school shootings, bullying, and stabbings which are now taking place in the schools and other venues, are but a few. That is the problem with cultural inherited hatred; it cannot be contained or directed to specific objects or people. This cultural inherited hatred spreads to every facet of your offspring's lives. This quality is a surprising result which never occurred to the white people who implement and practice this great idea. I do believe that President George W. Bush could have been a perfect man had he been given the opportunity to express his true spirituality. The first two Presidents were both spiritual Sevens and opposite in the type of victory they sought. President Lincoln's victory was done to save lives and correct a wrong. The fact that the Confederate Army would instead go to war for the right to continue raping and lynching innocent people was not President Lincoln's decision. The victory that President Bush sought was one that illustrated self-center actions and caused many unnecessary deaths. I do not claim to be exactly right on President Bush's background years as it refers to his family life, I recall the energy I would read on him from time to time from television.

The next is the 42nd President, Bill Clinton (1993 -2001). President Clinton's spiritual leadership path number is (4 + 2 = 6} is six. The definition for six has more layers than the others in a way. My life path number is six, so I have studied this one for a long time. Let me name some of the highest qualities; influenced by the Sun, beauty, and balance, compassion, harmony sought, and miracles. These people tend to be happy and fun to be around. They are usually very appealing in their physical looks, which draw much attention. They bring sunshine when entering the room. In the truest meaning of the word, these people tend to be very charismatic. In the mathematical world, six is considered a perfect number. Six's will be very magnetic to the opposite sex. People tend to hang onto every word. This quality can also leave room for trickery and underhanded actions on the part of a Six person. They can do a "trick of the hand" action on people, and the other will not catch it. Their charm causes people to watch the right hand when they should watch the left. They can be very spiritual and a good humanitarian, or the devil at the same time. President Clinton fit his spiritual leadership path number very well, I think. The Blacks seemed to like him because he appeared to be a friend. He smiled, ate soul food, kissed Black babies, and hugged us tightly. The real Clinton was extending prison sentences for the crimes Blacks would be charged. In fact, he proved to be a complete danger to our people, all the while smiling and hugging us. Because Clinton is a six and joined to the Sun, he would burn very bright. Also, just like the Sun, the six can burn too brightly and destroy themselves. We all remember the big affair scandal President Clinton gave us. It is not his fault, however, because he is by nature irresistible to all. Regardless, Bill is still very loved by the public. He still is the big charmer and brings the sunshine.

Age of Aquarius

The next is the 35th President, John F. Kennedy (1961-1963). His spiritual leadership path number (3 + 5 = 8) is eight. The fact that President Kennedy held this office exactly one hundred years after President Lincoln, is something that is very interesting. These two Presidents died for the same reasons. They were both trying to help a terrible wrong done to the African people. Some of the qualities of the eight are; influenced by Planet Mercury, splendor, majesty, strength, glory, endurance, and passionate expressions. In its spiritual awareness and conscious state, the eights are the direct fluid flow to the Creator. They seek justice while showing a strong sense of community and humanitarian involvement. I believe that President Kennedy did have an active compassion for community healing and wellness. He realized that the treatment of the Black people was at best, inhumane. I know for a fact that it was he who worked on the Bill of Rights with Dr. Martin Luther King, Jr., and other Civil Rights leaders. I know this because, during this early time in 1963, Dr. King, Jr., was in Americus GA, (my hometown) for our Civil Rights Movement. President Kennedy sent him there to come to the White House and work on the Bill. President Kennedy accepted his spirituality on this point and would do much for the Black people. He had determined to correct some of the injustices which Blacks endured. He was to start by getting the Bill of Rights passed and keep moving. However, another ruling faction in this Country decided this was not to be. I find it utterly uncanny that precisely one hundred years after President Lincoln was murdered for trying to help the Black community, President Kennedy was murdered for the same reason. What this shows is that the cultural inherited hatred traveled down time's highway unimpeded. It was just as strong and dangerous as before. Unfortunately, just as with President Lincoln, some people will kill to try and stop progress. Sadly, President Kennedy was dead before he could get this critical Bill passed. He was aware of the death threats against him for his Civil Rights action, but he decided to take a stand for justice. Again, the Heavenly Hosts had to step in and get the job done. The next President signed the Bill into law, but it was President Kennedy who should also be credited. Maybe this stand voided out some of his other transgressions. I certainly hope so.

The next selected is the 44th President, Barack Obama. His spiritual leadership path number (4 + 4=8) is eight. President Obama and President Kennedy share the number eight. Therefore, they had some of the same qualities and goals in mind. They both were strong humanitarians and believed in justice for all. Remember, that some of the levels for eight are as follows; influenced by Plant Mercury, splendor, glory, lovable, strength, passion, endurance, and majesty. These people will go the extra mile to get justice. President Obama's keen sense of the community and humanitarian good deeds were known throughout the Country and the world. He tried to balance the injustices of the government when it came to the consumers, health care, releasing prisoners from unjust sentences, on and on. I think he was the best President so far. The path of eights is usually a hard road. The spiritual people who attempt to do good or set things right, sometimes stir up much opposition. President Obama stirred up plenty of opposition with all he was doing. In the United States, the two main political parties fight like street people in expensive suits. President Obama, being a Black Democrat, had the horrific task of working with a majority white Republican Congress. A very high percentage of these officials were raised living with and exposed to cultural inherited hatred. The common name is segregation and white supremacy. I know I am right because I too was exposed to it as "white folks way of life." It is such a part of them and their offsprings, they do not realize that it exists. I learned a lot from my parents, community, school and all the other things I experienced growing up. The white people are no different. My world focused on specific goals, values, love and spirituality etc. So whites learn their world in the same way but different words and negativity. Let me make it entirely clear; this information does not include all white people. This dialog is about the believers of this hatred and practices it daily. They are people who have rejected the spirituality with which they were born to cause much trouble. You do not have to get everyone to participate. As I have learned, it only takes a few to cause untold misery. There are many things I experience from the actions of the white race that I do not understand. One of the main things is that they do not want you to call their prejudice and hate-filled actions what they are. Their behavior is one reason I label my study of them "white folk ology". They will usually call their actions everything but what they are. I guess that is one of their superior attitudes and way of thinking. They want us to pretend with them that they are good people. Another thing is how the Republican Congress and Representatives decided that they would band together during President Obama's term to make him a failure. Their lack of action is what I mean by cultural inherited hatred. This hatred originated at the beginning of this great Country. It rolled down the generational highway impacting and ensuring that this hatred would be kept alive. It is not of God. The white officials impeded the progress of this Country for eight years. The white Congress refused to fulfill their pledge and obligation to this nation only because the President was Black. They were not worried about a penalty for their inactivity and negative power move. They are the lawmakers and the highest in the land. How pitiful was their display? The best President ever was trying to do his job, and the elected officials told the citizens to kiss their asses. As a citizen, I think that they are a set of "big pussies." In other words, useless well-paid creeps. The officials were not prepared for the fallout, and sudden reduction in power after President Obama's term ended, however. This Age of Aquarius has the last word on what will be the outcome of their actions. The spiritual energy that is a ruler of this Age will be felt if not seen. To watch the missteps of the elected official day after day in Washington, D. C. is beyond anything imaginable. More on this in a later chapter. All I will say for now is that the Congress's negative response to President Obama is why we see what we do now. Spiritual energy will have the last word in real time now. Nonetheless, I do believe that President Obama was a sincere spiritual man. Because of his strong faith and enduring connection to the Creator, he was able to accomplish much in spite of their opposition. The most substantial impact of his legacy, I think, cannot be valued. It is beyond value because it deals with the happiest emotional aspect of life. His most precious election lifted our Will to the highest height ever. The height of energy and esteem that Blacks shared upon the election of President Obama cannot be measured here on earth. For me, this energy continues the heightened pride level experienced when I first met Dr. Martin Luther King, Jr. For our people, the story is this; we went from being free to be kidnapped; to being forced into slavery, to being somewhat restored. Our people are the actual "comeback kids." Our ancestors rejoice as they look down upon us. Just look at what we as a people have endured and overcome in America. Our Will to Live free will not stop. In summary, the two eights, Kennedy and Obama, were two men of strength and handsome. All the women who saw them would have gladly married either of them. They both had that "IT" factor, to me, they were of like minds, except that Kennedy loved the outside women openly. Obama appears to be happy with Michelle and loves her deeply.

The next to be examined is the 39th President, Lyndon B. Johnson (LBJ). His spiritual leadership path number (3 + 6 =9} is nine. Some of the more important qualities are; influenced by the Moon; it marks the completion of a cycle; A new cycle is birth; influences issues of foundation and judgment; can affect and change the emotional spheres of mankind; can be a bridge between spirituality and humanitarian acts. This type of person addresses major changes which could affect his leadership either negatively or positively. This is why it is a foundation and judgment influence most of all. President Johnson proves to be a man who addressed major foundation issues dealing with civil rights and segregation in this Country. He passed laws against discrimination in the workplace and other public facilities. He created Medicare and Medicaid. It seemed that he was a spiritual man and he wanted to set some things straight. He made a positive impact on raising people out of poverty in this Country. All of these things were changes in this Country's foundation. He made another foundation decision which ended up causing very negative effects. He put America deeper into the Vietnam War at a level the Country did not agree with. This was a bad judgment act. He caused another foundation change because his action tore the nation apart for years. I do not think that was his intent, he just did not understand the Vietnamese people and his actions failed. This foundation change has not completely healed even now. His other foundation changes were a success. He helps heal several issues positively for Blacks and other races. In that realm, President Johnson was very successful. I know the Heavenly Hosts guided his decisions. Maybe, he was just very spiritual and wanted to do the right thing. Either way, his presidency gave birth to a new cycle.

The next selected is the 45th, President Donald Trump (2017 - present). His spiritual leadership path number (4 + 5 = 9) is also nine. This is a Presidency still unfolding. Yet, after just one year, President Trump's world is in complete turmoil. Because he is nine, the foundation and judgment come into serious play now. To begin with, Trump was not supposed to win the presidency, according to the numbers reported before election day. In fact, no one was more surprised than he, of the win. Everyone could tell by his reaction that he was completely shocked about the win. I laughed because I understood why he won. I knew of the wind change a few years ago. I just did not know how the change would look. His followers want to believe that his election is a sign from God that he is a good leader. That is certainly not the case. The the moral characteristics this man shows (grabbing women pussies) is not something God agrees with. How could you be a true Christian and believe God would accept this man other than to be used to draw evil to him because like will travel together. As you can see, all the evil has come alive again. The people who support him are the example of the kind of inherited hatred kind. This is what "revealing" evil looks like and the people who do evil. The "less than-intelligent" Blacks who support him are just that, "less-than intelligent". President Trump is the catalyst for what is to happen related to this Age of Aquarius. His presidency will close down many negative cycles that are now being exposed through his world. The Holy Spirit will open more positive cycles. This is why you see all his dirty little secrets coming out. This intense spiritual energy present on earth denotes the change. All we have to do is notice the drastic change in the weather patterns. The dramatic increase in earthquakes and the unease of many things of nature. I have noticed these changes in many of my flowers. Will a major earthquake come and destroy our Country? Who knows for sure. Let us point out some qualities and attributes which could cause foundation changes for the current president. Since the 45th has been in the White House, he has caused some negative human foundation changes. The Republican Party is falling apart before our very eyes. The powers that be are unable to stop its demise because the cycle of the current Party is changing. The people who practice the cultural inherited hatred believed his election to be a signal to increase expression of hatred towards the other races. The whites see this as a signal to increase the purchase of more guns to be used against those they hate. The 45th is the catalyst that has shaken the Republicans. The party foundation has been destroyed by his inability to lead. The 45th is the catalyst for the increased tension between the races. The 45th is the catalyst for why the Nations around the world now see us as a joke. The 45th has no problem making an ass of himself, thereby, making the world

Age of Aquarius

think we are crazy for electing him; the 45th is the reason the world governments do not trust what we say. The 45th is a man whose character is missing spirituality. The 45th continually lies to Congress and the American people. I am going to say that he will not make the four years as president. The mental issues he is now having will show itself shortly. The one true sign will be a total public meltdown for everyone to see. The 45th is almost at that point even as I write this book. The foundation shaking the 45th is currently doing will not serve this Country well, at first. The Age of Aquarius spiritual energy will dictate how this period will play out on a more positive cycle. The Cosmos is going through significant change right now, and these changes will show themselves on earth. Just be ready for the unexpected. I am sure many people can feel the energy shifts occurring at this time. I know I can. The one thing no one knows is what each strange occurrence means. As we can see, the two nines are similar in that they change the foundation of the Country. The difference being President Johnson's changes were positive, and the current 45th President is out for destruction and failure. Judgment will follow in this Age.

For the sake of history, let us examine the 37th President, Richard Nixon, (1969-1974). President Nixon's spiritual leadership number (3+7 = 10) is ten. The material plane, earth always influences this number. Ten in the material world means the exposure and subsequent death of a hidden idea or action, usually not positive. These exposures cause the beginning of new paths. Ten is reduced to one and that means new actions. The Watergate scandal certainly emphasizes this principle. President Nixon and his Party were discovered during such an action, trying to scam the American people. Careers ended and President Nixon resigned to start over in another career. The Age of Aquarius is the cleansing age. There will be a lot of things brought to the boiling point which will cause massive changes.

The strong spiritual energy will not be denied. If we choose to be spiritual, this energy will make you stronger. You will be able to connect to the Highest source and accomplish things you never knew were there. As it stands right now, the Republican Congress is at a loss as to how to handle these situations the 45th has created for them. He has them looking quite stupid and they are unable to stop the destruction, it seems. Suddenly, they are not feeling superior and this frightens them. As a child, I was told about this time and how things would be. So, I am watching and thinking just as the Sages taught me. The 45th's purpose in this part of the story is to evoke both negative as well as stronger positive emotions, which are surfacing rapidly. What is happening now, can easily be compared to the type of strong emotions leading up to the Civil War. The 45th is the catalyst for division and disharmony. He is also the catalyst for spiritual energy that conquers and guide those who will come to know the truth about his actions. The impact of this spiritual energy and deep emotion will be felt by all. The result is that each individual will have to make a decision as to what side to take. The spiritual energy that is covering us now will cleanse each of us and we will have to go right or left. Will we as a civilization hate or love? People will have to decide to be spiritual and express it or not. The Heavenly Hosts demand balance and the universe is not at all balanced, right now. We are not being shown all that is going on with the citizenry of our Country. As a result, we cannot counteract the real causes to help stop the negative outbursts occurring right now. All one can discern is that white people are running scared of the other races, so they are buying guns by the hundreds. Why are they scared or frightened, no one can say because I am certain they still think of themselves as superior.

White Folkology

White folkology is a term I coined to study white folk and their behavior, actions, beliefs, and overall thought processes. I started this study when I began ninth grade at the newly integrated high school in my small hometown in 1965. I had to understand how people could hate me for no reason. I continued this study all throughout life. It has helped a great deal knowing what I do about them. The fact that this Country is still a young one, we can study its history from the very beginning with accuracy, for the most part. We can certainly see how society and government developed to the level they are now. The cultural inherited hatred began to form in its current state at the end of the Civil War. There are just too many white men who want to continue their evil practices on Blacks, regardless of what the law said. So they formed groups to proceed with the raping, killing, lynching, and tormenting the "freed" people of Africa. This should have been expected, however, because the North and South had completed a brutal war where brother fought against brother, and the South lost. Why were they fighting this unbelievable horrific war? One brother wanted to stop the slave trade and the other brother wanted to continue raping, humiliating, selling, and tormenting the "freed" slaves. Why the hate though. The whites who participated in the slave trade convinced themselves that what they were doing was not wrong, oh but it was. The evil and negative energy produced during this time did not go unnoticed by God. The fact that the founding fathers lied by calling their acts sanctioned by God is not going to be unnoticed. What happened to the evil energy and the cries of the victims? It is a question which has not been answered, until now. At the time of the slave trade, not much was known by the white man about human energy. My grandma knew that the energy and soul of the killed kidnapped Africans were still present. She often spoke about seeing them. Especially the souls who had refused to cross over because of their anger. She would often say, "I wonder when they will make themselves known"? I asked what she meant. She would say something like the souls have a purpose and they would not leave until the time has come. She said that she would not see the end of this drama but that I would see the beginning. The time is close to the end of this man-made drama. The Age of Aquarius is now here in full effect and the unseen souls will make themselves known to many. I often wonder what did the whites think would happen to the human soul/energy as a result of their evil actions. To live in this world and think we are all there is to existence is downright silly. But if you are taught that men are in control of all things, you have to believe what they say. Until very recently, the white race was under the belief of "religion" as explained by their leaders. Religion, as being taught by most white leaders, is a catch all control situation that favors the leadership. Everything is done in the name of God, so people don't question what is said. People can only tell you what it is they know. If their scope is limited, then that which is spoken will be limited. The whites never thought that anything would happen as a result of their evil actions. There was no immediate negative comeback, so they kept on as usual. They were not worried because their actions were sanctioned by the United States government. The whites felt that no one could stop them and they could do any and everything they wanted to the Africans. In March 2018, a survey was taken with the white population here in the United States. It was discovered that whites fear Blacks the most and are preparing for an encounter, a race war if you please. What would be the purpose of such a war, I wonder? They are buying more and more guns because of their fear of us. That sounds so much like the "white folkology" I speak about. Why, is a question that any sane person would ask. I believe they are afraid because deep down in their soul, they know it was wrong to try and make us slaves to them. I know that the Holy Spirit is working on their spirits. Since the entry of kidnapped African into the United States, whites have terrorized, humiliated, stolen from us, jailed us, raped us, killed us, etc., all in the name of their Christian rights granted by the cultural inherited hatred. The Creator is not happy how he is being prostituted in the fake religion world. All the Blacks wanted was to be left alone to express themselves and recover from the dark period of slavery. It actually takes a while for such a recovery of a people to show balance. The fear whites are now feeling is justified because they created the evil elements which got us to this point in history. Whites are unaware that love and hate are the same life highway. The difference is that with love you are going forward and with hate, you are traveling backward. In conclusion my white people of hate and disgust, you have but your forefather to blame for all your woes. If only they had not been so greedy, evil, and determined with the destruction of others type people. Maybe, you would have a better America. As we can now see by the crumbling of this phase to our story, their choice to hate was not a good one.

Age of Aquarius Spiritual Energy

The spiritual energy present today is what will rule the day. It is the Holy Spirit itself that is here and it rules the spiritual energy. To be perfectly honest, the Creator is tired of so much hatred and is going to do something big about it. When we study the history of past known civilizations, we are better able to see how societies develop. Regardless of what man creates and/or magnificent objects invented, it is the energy (will) of the humans and the Astrological influences which dictates how we will exist. Because America is such a young civilization, it is easy to trace events and see how our society exists as it does today. At this time in man's history, we are better able to understand the connection between us and the Heavenly Hosts. The ancient people had a better understanding, but the knowledge somehow got buried. Time has come for mankind to do a more magical and mysterious way of thinking about life. The Holy Spirit is here for that reason. The traditional ways of understanding the Holy Spirit will be elevated to levels never before seen. We have to raise our consciousness to meet this spiritual energy through receiving the Holy Spirit. Many people are sensing something energy-related and don't know how to define it or what is happening. The spiritual energy Is very strong and determined to communicate with us. We need to start recognizing the different energetic feelings and get in touch with our spirituality. There has always been spirituality long before there was religion. At some point in time, some person(s), realizing how powerful spirituality was, decided to turn as much as they could into "religion." The religious leaders quickly learned that religion was a very effective way to control the masses. Also, it is a great way to acquire a great deal of wealth. Of course, greed sets in and all the rest is history which we can now see. Realizing that time is measured differently in the Cosmos, mankind seems to be realizing what has happened and redirecting this mistake made by religious leaders hundreds of years ago. More and more people want the true spirituality given by the Holy Spirit. This need makes them seek new leaders of the truth. The imbalance caused by this error in religion by man, demands a correction by the Cosmos. This Age of Aquarius will bring about cleansing and correction in the realm of religion. People are already awakening to the need to do the right thing. The "same old same old" is not going to work now. One has to think of Noah and his spiritual mission at this time. I wonder how long had the people of his world been "misbehaving" when Noah received his charge from the Creator? How old was this area where Noah lived? The Bible does not give any indication other than it had been going on for some time. The people in America have been "misbehaving" for just a few hundred years, so, are we close to a major change? I know we are at that time in history for major change. With each new Age, a major change will occur. Is there a Noah for us or will the change just appear? The manner in which America was created does not add up to good fortune for us. The evil which formed America and has continued until today will be dealt with by this Holy Spirit. Nothing is forgotten due to the length of time that has passed. There has been no reconciliation for many past wrongs. Every day that passes, we discover more and more evil. The old "cause and effect" thing will make corrections. I do not accept the theory that man could do anything he wishes and the Creator will learn to live with it. Some have said that America will never face judgment for all the injustices she has done to many innocent people. Those people will be wrong, of course. The spirit of the enslaved people still live and will not be ignored by the Holy Spirit. The Bible teaches us that "man can kill the body but not the spirit (soul)," Is that true or not? I know it to be accurate and have seen strong will overcome much and be victorious. There was a poll taken in early 2018 and it showed that a large majority of whites fear Blacks. Why are the whites afraid of us? Well, it could be the nightmares that they recently began having. In their dreams, they are persecuted by images of spirits seeking revenge for slavery and other evil deeds. If they have not started dreaming, there is a small voice in the back of their minds which is causing the fear. I recall when I realized it had started happening to them, just a few years ago, and I wondered how they would accept it. Of course, they started buying more guns. The thing about the Holy Spirit, however, is that it can prevent the gun from firing. I wondered how that would play into this story and now I see. All you have to do is ask white people about these dreams and it will be stated as such. I have never ask, myself, because I know what they dream. I am told about dreams through my energy and connection to the universe. Hidden knowledge is very clear to me and can be that way to others. This is the Age to receive such "knowing". This is the Age spoken of in the Bible where people will dream of prophecy and become more enlightened. By that, I mean that spirituality is in the air we breathe. This spiritual energy has made many people understand what the Bible really says. There are people who have the knowledge and they don't know what to do with it. This is a new Age and all the people have not opened up their subconscious senses yet. The whites who fear us are experiencing a "tug of war" in their souls, and this is what causes their alarm. Not to mention, the fact that all their lives have been spent hating for no reason. To hate help makes them feel powerful. This feeling is getting ready to make a U-turn, and they are somehow aware of this. Again, I ask why the hate? Why not want to do the right and just thing? The spirit and soul is very powerful and they can take over your body. Spiritual healing is as powerful as the emotion of love. The time has arrived when the Creator will make himself known in a very loud manner. Just pay attention to the undefinable weather changes we are having in all the areas of America. The Creator speaks through his creation, and we need to listen. There are apparent words being spoken through the unexpected things we see. Then we need to ask the universe what she means by this? Whenever there is an unforeseen change in the Cosmos (weather), then there will be an unpredictable change on earth. Man will and is experiencing things that were not able to be predicted. Life is changing and the whites who hate and fear us are going to find out that their way will not be as easy as before. Their people are not alongside them as they were in the past. There are large numbers of whites who are now enlightened and refuse to hate in such ways. They know there is a better way for humanity to take. Their spirituality is leading their consciousness. No, no I am not saying that all the races are going to stand together and sing, I am just saying it will not be as it was. People will find authentic ways to co-exist and make a better world. Every day we hear about people taking a stand against what they know is wrong and making demands for respectability. In any phase of society, there are push backs and the "good old boys" did not see it coming. They were broadsided and didn't have a proper response. The inactivity makes them lose grounds and influence. The society of America is experiencing an earthquake, and there is no class at any of the universities to explain how to handle it. I believe spiritual energy is attacking all negative energies and winning. In the words of a great man, Sam Cook, a change is going to come". The Moon will not leave this realm, is one of the things astrologers have noticed. The presence of the Moon always has a massive impact on man's behavior. Remember that the 45th President is a Nine (Moon) and the two together have great significance. The people in America will have to line up with the right or the wrong sides very soon. Let us loosely examine what has happened so far. The 45th Presidency has really put some things in the fast lane. The Congress which hatefully blocked Obama's Presidency for eight years, now found themselves completely powerless to deal with the 45th President. The Republican party finds itself being torn apart because of the 45th

President's action and lack of leadership skills. Some Republicans are trying to stick with the president, some Republicans don't want to be associated with the president, and still, others are simply being silent about all he does. His acts are so not like a president, the entire world laughs at him. The "usual" acts of the 45th President, in my most humble opinion, are not accepted by some party members. The Republican Party is supposed to be the party for family, honor, religion, and other such ideals is what I have always heard them say. These ideals have not been mentioned once since the 45th President came on the scene. Family values cannot be mentioned with this presidency because it does not exist. This 45th President has been married three times, cheated on all his wives and now that he is President, his playmate porno stars are suing him. Although we are talking about a loosely knit family with all his outside activity, it is not the one the Republicans had in mind. These kinds of happenings cannot do their party any good. Now you have different groups in the Republican Party having public "pissing" contests. Neither group wants to make their district unhappy and neither district seems to have all the same goals. The fact that the Republicans can't prevent the 45th President from making blunder after blunder with the presidency, makes them look stupid and less powerful. This is a great example of what karma looks like for them after "playing dead" for eight years when President Obama was in office. They did not see this chain of events coming and again, they have no response ready. Something else which will be on-going about the "good old boys" club. The white women have finally started to speak out about the abuse they suffer from their powerful white man. The outcry is something that the white man has never experienced before. They usually have control over what the white woman says and does. White women, until recently, seems to have been raised to stand by their man regardless as to what he does to you. I would see the wives of powerful men standing in the background while her husbands apologize for one affair after another. I thought to myself, what a horrid position for a wife to be. For her to stand there humiliated by what her husband says, is nothing but abuse. Then I think, well at least she gets to live well and only has to compromise her integrity and dignity. Black women received nothing during the slavery years when white men raped and humiliated us. The unwanted sexual behavior shown by the white man is an excellent example of how white men do not change. I guess that the white women thought that a man would control his evil and not direct it at her. "Evil is as evil does" is in any man. If he did it to one woman, he would do it to you eventually. What was the point that caused the white ladies to break their long-guarded secrets of sex abuses? Why at this point and time in history did they all want their stories heard? What made them say enough is enough? I think that because we are well in the Age of Aquarius, it was not their call. More and more negative and positive revelations will come forth all over concerning hidden evil. The spiritual energy present now is what drives such truths to be told. It was not the white woman's call, the Heavens made them speak all at once. When the Universe speaks to us, you will respond. Just as when it suddenly starts to rain, you respond by seeking shelter. This was another unforeseen revelation which the good old boys had no prepared response for. White men have always been in control of the society, which meant that their women accepted whatever and kept their mouths closed. Not to worry, however, white men are somewhere now planning a comeback, of that I am sure. Please do not think that these sexual evils have stopped being practiced. I feel they have just changed their tactics and ways of doing things. Just as it is in the religious institutions which are plagued by major sex abuse scandals have not stopped what they do. Sexual addiction is as real as the drug problems in this world.

Age of Aquarius Energy and You

Time is the great equalizer, a great saying. I like it most because change will happen just as I know it will. The time has finally arrived, and the world will be made equal in the ways that matter. The spiritual energy will balance out this world. I will not be here for the entire 2500 years of this Age; I can rest assured, however, knowing that the change will take place. The righteous people will take their proper place, and the wrong will not go free. Fortunately, I will get to see quite a bit of the change. They are happening while I am watching right now. The honorable Queen Winnie Mandela went to her Heavenly throne today. She is a designated warrior along with women like my grandma, mother and Maa Dove. Things are about to get interesting shortly. The spiritual energy is about to burst out from every angle. People who never knew about the Creator will seek him out. The churches are going to be judged for the wrongdoing which is currently going on. There will be a demand for a better presentation of the Creator's love caused by this spiritual energy. People like Oprah Winfrey have the correct idea when it comes to the new expression of spirituality. The current religious institutions are marketed as a "one-man show" and all the money is for them. Men have preached the story of "men only" for so long, they will be shocked when this new spirituality take hold. Of course, there will be men who speak very negatively about the new ways. Nothing can be said about that because a change is still coming whether they welcome it or not. Women are fed up with so many things which have put them on a crusade path not yet known to them. The more the white men continue to recklessly kill the Black men does nothing but make the Black woman's strongest side surface. Black women were very dangerous during slavery and nothing was off limits when it came to their children and family. A killing was nothing new when they could manage it. They were forced into those life-threatening situations and they tried to help. All kinds of secrets were held back from us systematically, for good reason. But there is always someone left to tell the story. Black people mastered a silent language during slavery because the white man denied them to speak to each other. Think of Harriet Tubman and how, as a Black woman, she led many slaves to freedom. She relied on the guidance of her ancestors and the Holy Spirit. This was a huge move by a former slave. Intelligence is from the Creator and not man. The white man, with all his control devices, could not stop her. She managed this without talking to the slaves. They could read her energy and understood they should follow her. The woman is the preserver of the races and this spiritual energy is present and we will awaken. We will do the same thing again now that it has become necessary. The fear whites have for us started during the captured Africans period because it did not take them long to discover that we were not the stupid people they had claimed. We just spoke a different language. The 45th President is a great inspiration to his loyal followers. This president is a Nine, more on that later. Therefore, evil is running rampant and out of control. He has inspired the KKK (one of the oldest known white hate groups) to kill all who are not white. In the twist of fate way, more whites who hate are shooting their peers at work, school, social gatherings, etc. These two situations are related because whites have been taught to hate all their lives. Some white people choose not to express their hatred in public, but they still do it in secret ways. White men seem to be suffering from a hefty dose of inhumanity. I often wondered how do white women love the men who worship and hate. Then I remember how white women are raised to follow the white man regardless of how he behaves. The number nine has many aspects to it. The Moon influences it. The Moon can be a way to elevate the darker side as well. It is considered to be a completion of a cycle and brings in a new one. The new sequence is what is happening right now in our lifetime. The nine is associated with our reproduction system in that it takes nine months for a baby to complete the birth cycle and then it comes into the new setting, Earth.

Holy Spirit Equals Spirituality

There cannot be spirituality without receiving the Holy Spirit. The Holy Spirit has always been present even before Jesus arrived. In fact, it was the Holy Spirit which covered Mary and she became pregnant with the baby Jesus, or so the Bible says. Many great people have declared that "greed" will be the death of mankind, and they could be right. The Holy Spirit seems to be very unhappy with the ways our human race is going. The atmosphere is buzzing with the high energy of the Holy Spirit. Just as there is a downside to our history of slavery, there is a worse downside to freedom with no limits or moral compass. The "powers that be" are in a downfall right now because of their endless pursuit of all that is wrong. This "too much society", in which a lot of the controlling race exist, is an expression of how this thing happens. In the fifties, I saw a movie in which Bettye Davis said "I am young, white, and free" when someone tried to prevent her from doing something. The saying had a powerful meaning and made a statement of how whites felt and continue to feel. Mostly it made it clear that anything and everything seems to be the motto of the century for the white race. This type of scenario can only be brought into play when the people who are in control have no fear of reprisals and/or punishment. Who decides what is wrong or right? Actually, the Holy Spirit does. Each of the controlling generations, since the beginning of America, has become filled with more greed than the generation before. They think they have evolved, but in actuality, they are devolving. Greed is one of the most deadly sins. Become very comfortable in their way of acting and thinking because hundreds of years have passed and they have not felt the wrath of the Holy Spirit in the way that is coming. Just as it was our ancestors who suffered their harshness.

It will be their descendants. Just as the people who were destroyed in the story of Noah or other cities, all the ones who constructed evil died before the punishment came. Their descendants received the payback. In the Bible, it is referred to as "sins of the father". To never have limits sets man up for self-destruction every time. The white race in America certainly fit that bill. The Holy Spirit will take over at some point and make corrections. This balancing act is taking place in our time. I have always prayed to the Creator to allow me this moment. I will not see it all. I'm glad to see whatever I can. Just like the people in Noah's time, the white race does not believe they will be punished. I do not know how long the imbalance had been going on before Noah was chosen but it took him one hundred and twenty years to build his boat. This much time passing made the sinners feel safe and doubt what he told them. When the Holy Spirit gave the word, the end happened. Regardless of your station in life, you need to get in touch with the Holy Spirit. It is humanity's only hope in this trying time. We are going to experience something huge in the way of life changes very soon. We need to rise to the occasion. The old way of serving and honoring the Creator is over. The Creator wants us to go to a higher level and meet with him. In my opinion, the churches and the religious institutions have dulled the senses of too many people. We have to "look behind the curtains" as my grandma would say. Humanity should be exploring the mysteries behind the words we read in the Bible. Seeking a deeper meaning is where the Holy Spirit can help. It can open your "third eye" to reveal an elevation of power and miracles which the Creator has for us. We have all we need when we receive the Holy Spirit in our day-to-day lives in all that we do. The Age of Aquarius is all about the Holy Spirit coming to Earth for 2000+ years. Sorry, I will not see the end of this Age nor how humanity would have evolved.

Astrology and Spiritual Belief

Here, I want to show in more detail how the Bible connects the dots of the Ages that I can identify. As I stated earlier, there is a solid connection between the Bible and Astrology. I hope my following explanation will prove this to all. As I understand it, Abraham and Sarah were called out of their homelands by the Holy Spirit. Clearly, there was an old civilization existing long before Abraham was given his mission, becoming the Spiritualist. I wonder how old was Abraham's world when Abraham and Sarah were sent out by God? Had the people in his world become so corrupt and out of the will of God that God felt it was time to intervene and save his people, yet again. The Spiritualist Abraham introduces the concept of the One True God. It was at this time the Creator decided to show His LOVE for His creation. I would label this period as the Age of Gemini because it is the introduction and uniting of God and man into a single mindset of love. Gemini is known as the Lovers card in tarot, The Age of Gemini was all about love and trying to make humanity understand the Creator's love for his creation. The pleading and passionate love shown by Abraham to God in trying to save the people of Sodom and Gomorrah from destruction is a strong display of love. Remember how Abraham was going to kill his only child to prove his love for God and God saved the son because of His love for Abraham. Abraham did many acts of love all throughout his time. "ALL ABOUT THE LOVE" IS WHAT THE AGE OF GEMINI EXPRESSES.

The next is the Age of Taurus and Moses was the vessel, the Hierophant. The Spiritualist who delivered the word of the God. Moses' name has five letters which make him VAV in the name of the Creator. He took the spoken word to Egypt Pharaoh so the Jews would go free and to show the power of the Creator. In Egypt is where the ten plagues were, and finally, the Pharaoh gave in. Taurus the Bull was in full effect. I do believe that this period was at the end of the Age of Taurus because of Moses's reaction upon returning to his people. When Moses returned to the people after a long time away period, he found they had made the golden oxen, bull, or calf, to worship. He was angry and told them that this was wrong because this Age is passing and a new mindset is present. He was getting people ready for the arrival of Jesus in the next Age, Age of Aries.

Next is the Age of Aries. The time for the Ram of God to arrive. At what point in this Age did Jesus enter is not clear. It is just made clear that He was the Ram of God declared in previous times. The Ram is the sign for Aries. When Jesus was here, He made some references to the end of the Age. This reference to Ages meant He was signaling His awareness of the different Astrological Ages. More than once, in the Bible, Jesus referred to the fact that He would be with the disciples until the end of the Age. There was much confusion as to what Jesus meant by these words. The disciples first thought that Jesus meant until the end of the world. This thought changed after the death of Jesus on the cross, and they did not know what was happening. He had also told the disciples that He would return. They believed Jesus would return soon or at least in their lifetime. This caused confusion among his disciples because they thought Jesus meant until the end of the world. When Jesus died, they were not clear about what would happen next. The disciples believed that the end of the world was coming after Jesus' death. His reappearance after His death caused them further confusion. I think Jesus died at the end of Age of Aries and reappeared to His disciples at the beginning of the Age of Pisces. The length of the Age is the reason that people say "Jesus died some 2000 years ago". The is now the end of the Age of Pisces.

The Age of Pisces is represented by the fish. In the Bible Jesus is associated with the fish. The famous magical feeding of the five a

Age of Aquarius

thousand with a few fish is just one example. Jesus was known as the fisher of men. His disciples continued this work after He went to Heaven. The Age of Pisces is now behind us but has left its fingerprints. What was the role of the Age of Pisces in the Spiritual expression happening now? The time of religion and control through the religious world has drawn the attention of the Holy Spirit. The arrival, in part, is because of all the misrepresentation presented by the religious leaders. I am sure back at the beginning of this Age; the leaders had good intentions. Just as in everything else, the further we got from the start the more comfortable it became to do evil by all. The "greed bug" bit them all. Now, it seems that to align with the Creator, one has to become a Spiritualist. Thankfully, there are Spiritualist leaders who know all about the knowledge I seek. I could speak on the just ended Age of Pisces which was incredibly wrong and evil, but I won't go into detail. We have already seen a lot of the wicked happenings which we will continue seeing for a while. The spiritual way which was freely given by the Creator to us has been unmercifully misused and abused causing more harm than good, is what brings the Holy Spirit to us at this time. WHO WILL ANSWER THE CALL?

Here we are now in the great Age of Aquarius. This Age is intellectual, positive, scientific, masculine, metaphysical, spiritual, philosophical. balance and corrective in a humanitarian manner, just to name a few of its vibrations. How is the Holy Spirit going to respond to what is happening on earth? Boy, we do have clues, like the volcanic eruption now occurring in Hawaii and other places, the earthquakes all over the world, the increased hatred displayed by the police, the significant drastic weather changes, just to name a few. The world seemed to be crumbling all around us. The uninformed people who think that business will be as usual is so wrong in their assessment. Maa Sis (my grandma) would always say, "just because it is this way today, does not mean it will be that way tomorrow." Consider the people of Pompeii, Noah's time, and

Sodom and Gomorrah. I am sure they went to bed the night before the end with no ideas as to what would happen to their world within a few hours. Since America is such a young nation, it is easy to see how the past has shaped our future. The "powers that be" have played gods for so long, they now are comfortable that they will dictate the rest of our future. You see, they feel they are superior even unto the Creator. Whenever there are no limits in a society, i.e., the white world, it will self-destruct with all the unchecked freedom. If the white race is so angry with the Blacks, they have only their forefathers to blame. Their forefathers should never have done such a "redistribution of wealth" of the African people. Greed will always cause self-destruction. They have become wealthy because of their actions but lost their humanity. The Holy Spirit is here now and who will be left standing. I have often wondered what would this world be if the whites had not been raised to hate. I do not know if this type of hate development in another Country exists. I am referring to whether any other Country has worshiped and built their foundation on hate as America continues to practice.

Finally, for this part, I love that a beautiful Black woman is now the Duchess after she has married a handsome Duke in England as of May 19, 2018. The wind has changed at the top for the best. I am amazed every day at what is happening in America, and I will write more in book two. The information from the other realm is coming quickly.

SPIRITUAL RECKONING HAS BEGUN

When I wrote this book in 2017, I was not expecting that the actions would be so swift and overwhelmingly high in the number of people and organizations rebuking the religious establishments.

The energy levels and intensity have increased tremendously within the past seven years. Seven years ago, I felt the change in energy and knew that this Age of Aquarius was in full effect. With that being said, I knew all would be revealed for every cultural activity there is. Think of how our society is having too much difficulty in the cultural world as it is right now. The various issues, abortion, gay pride, race relations, drug abuse, sexual abuse, increased killings over minor things, etc.

The fact that all that we see and not see is energy based must be established. We are a form of energy, furniture is a form of energy, food is a form of energy, etc. With these facts stated we must appreciate and acknowledge that the Earth's energy is very much impacted by the major source of energy, the Universe. The fact that the Universe was created by the Creator makes the Creator the ultimate source of energy. This is our connection to the Creator with which all living things are ensured. This connection cannot be broken, only misused.

The strength and power level of such energy in living things are only determined by the Creator. The level of understanding of said energy is also determined by the Creator. In some humans this understanding is so powerful that we are able to comprehend the true meaning of things and do not have to rely on others for a higher wisdom. My grandma would say "it's in your bloodline." She taught me many things about the unseen realm and how to read the heavenly bodies and their actions, movements. I speak of my Great Grandmother, whom I never met but have since felt her presence. She was a woman born into slavery. Without formal education she was able to teach my grandma things that were not taught to her. She had inherited this knowledge. I am living proof that slavery did not impede the knowledge of the Creator. Although the white man had changed our physical existence, they could not stop the true existence of knowledge.

I was brought up in the church and read the bible, I still knew that true wisdom and knowledge could be gained through other means. I could not rely on the word coming from the mouth of a man calling himself a preacher. My mother was truly a Godly and Spiritual woman who had been born from a woman who had the same kind of inherited knowledge in her bloodline as my grandma. My father's mother lived next door. She helped me to understand my other grandma's communication with me.

My childhood was perfect and filled with happiness. The out of the world knowledge I received and lived was the best. I knew that I was always loved and cherished. Mother was a stay-at-home mom and she spoiled all six of us. She and I did have a special "unworldly" connection, however. I always watched and observed everything about her. Eventually, I became the teacher and she the student. My mother's mother died when my mother was six months old yet the communication between them never stopped. I would see my mother's lips moving and finally ask her why she did that. She laughed and said, "you pay too close attention to me". I am speaking with your grandma, my mother. I asked her how that was done if grandma was dead. She said she did not know but that ever since she was a child, it had been happening. Mother said, this made her not miss her so much as a child. When my mother began having her six children, communication was every day. This made me know that slavery stopped nothing when it came to the Creator. Although, I do not understand why the Creator allowed this horrible thing to happen to my people. Maybe one day I will be told, I have asked many times.

My grandma lived in the house next door to ours with me learning all I could from her. Trust me, she had a lot to say and do in our community. Please read my other book, Merritt Magic, to find out more about her. Grandma and I spent many hours looking at the stars when I was growing up, among many other things. In the country, the sky was always clear and the objects very visible. She was able to explain the significant shapes and location of the importance of their placement. She taught me the importance of the Dog star and how to find and follow it. This is major. Nothing like it probably was in the big cities. I am so happy I grew up in a small town in GA. This is also the reason I love Astrology, the unknown and the like.

Now to the current world. There is going to be an important eclipse on April 8, 2024. Seven years after the other major eclipse on August 21, 2017. For those of you who have not been following the events of the religious world, that eclipse was the telling of the coming reveal of the evils of this world. Look around and see how much and how many leaders in that religious world have fallen. Too many to count. So many of the leaders who have not been exposed yet are leaving that world on an hourly basis. They are openly declaring their departure which is completely new in that world.

The energy from that eclipse was so strong and powerful that no one could run from it and many did not know what was happening to them. Some still are in the dark about the energy impact and destruction. Luckily for me, I did know what was happening. In fact, I knew before it happened. My mother and grandmother had explained it to me before their death. The religious world will never recover from what has happened. A new Spiritual world is going to emerge. People are searching for the truth which can only be found through Spirituality.

The Catholic church will fall next. It is too corrupt to stand. If one pays attention, it has already begun. The lie that the church was built on Peter is the first lie, which means it was built on an unsolid foundation. Peter never started that organization. It stands on death and destruction. Just read the history of that church and it becomes clear.

The Catholics have another serious problem, it is built on masculine energy alone. This means there is no balance, just male energy. The world does not operate like this. If feminine energy was not required, then women would not be needed, thereby, men would have babies and run the business. This creation is built on a dual energy principle and no man can successfully change it. The Creator is all about balance. This will be the major negative issue against the organization. Let us watch to see if I am correct or not.

The prosperity churches are just as bad. The saving grace for them is their existence is shorter than the Catholic organization. Thank the Creator for that point. The fact that we now live in an Age where all things will be revealed helps me to know certain things. The veil has been lifted and things are more easily understood. When questions enter the mind, the answer is right behind the thought. This is a new thing for some people who knew nothing about the veil. The good thing is now they become aware of other worlds. The awakening can be scary, alarming or misunderstood.

You hear all kinds of predictions about what is going to happen next by all sorts of individuals. Please do not think about what they say too closely. They know nothing. No one knows what is next, we can only wait to see. I do know that Spirituality expression is going to take a GIANT STEPFORWARD. I will not see the entire transformation, but I am comforted to see the beginning.

I have enjoyed my travels through this existence and am happy about it.

Age of Aquarius

I lost my mother in 1993, but I talk to her just as she talked to her mother. This is the Age of Aquarius and magic is everywhere. Magic is one of Aquarius's gifts to mankind. You have but to know that it does. Mental thought of the highest Spiritual nature is all that is required. Be ready for you to have Spiritual experiences. MOST OF ALL, GIVE THANKS TO THE CREATOR AND RESPECT THE CREATION.

www.ingramcontent.com/pod-product-compliance
Lightning Source LLC
LaVergne TN
LVHW040159080526
838202LV00042B/3230